MAKING SHAPES

© Aladdin Books Ltd 1995

Created and produced by NW Books
28 Percy Street, London W1P OLD

First published in the United States by
Copper Beech Books, an imprint of
The Millbrook Press
2 Old New Milford Road
Brookfield, Connecticut 06804

Editor: Jon Richards

Design:
David West Children's Book Design
Designer: David Millea
Illustrator: Tony Kenyon
Photography: Roger Vlitos
Models: David Millea

Printed in Belgium

Library of Congress Cataloging-in-Publication Data
Gibson, Gary. 1957-
Making Shapes / by Gary Gibson : illustrated by Tony Kenyon.
p. cm. -- (Science for Fun)
Includes index.
Summary: Includes instructions for and explanations of
experiments that introduce such topics as elasticity,
tessellation, fibers, and bridges.
ISBN 1-56294-631-5 (lib. bdg. : alk paper)
1. Structural engineering--Experiments--Juvenile
literature. 2. Science--Experiments--Juvenile literature.
[1. Science—Experiments. 2. Experiments.]
I. Kenyon, Tony. ill. II. Title. III. Series: Gibson, Gary
1957-   Science for Fun.
TA634.G53   1995   95-10817
624.1'078--dc20   CIP AC

SCIENCE
FOR FUN

MAKING
SHAPES

GARY GIBSON

COPPER BEECH BOOKS
Brookfield, Connecticut

CONTENTS

INTRODUCTION **5**

MYSTERIOUS SHAPES **6**

SHAPES IN NATURE **8**

HANGING ROCKS **10**

SHAPE AND STRENGTH **12**

HANGING AROUND **14**

MAKING MATERIALS **16**

FILLING SHAPES **18**

ELASTIC MATERIALS **20**

SHAPELESS PLASTICS **22**

FIBERS AND THREADS **24**

FITTING IT TOGETHER **26**

BRIDGES **28**

FANTASTIC SHAPE FACTS **30**

GLOSSARY **31**

INDEX **32**

INTRODUCTION

You may have walked across a bridge and wondered how it was able to support your weight, and the weight of bicycles, cars, and trucks. Objects around us assume a variety of shapes and sizes, depending on the job that they must do. How does the shape of an egg make it strong? How are stalactites formed? How does a spring keep its shape, and how can plastic lose its shape? This book contains a selection of exciting "hands-on" projects to help answer some of these questions.

When this symbol appears, adult supervision is required.

MYSTERIOUS SHAPES

We can learn a lot about materials and their shapes from nature. All of these shapes are solids, and have at least two sides. What about a one-sided shape? What special properties does it have?

MAKE A MÖBIUS STRIP

1 Color both sides of three paper strips. Tape together the first strip to make a band.

2 Repeat with the second strip, but twist the strip once before sticking the ends together.

WHY IT WORKS

The first strip will make two new bands, the second a single long band and the third, two linked bands. This is a trick of mathematics. The second and third strips are called *Möbius strips*, after their inventor.

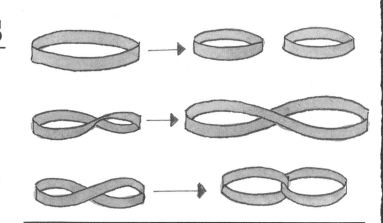

3 Twist the third strip twice before taping the ends together.

4 Finally, cut each band in half lengthwise.

FURTHER IDEAS

Draw a pencil line along each of the bands. You will find that the line continues along both "sides" of the second band!

SHAPES IN NATURE

You can find crystals everywhere around you. Gemstones, like emeralds, have always fascinated people. Salt, sand, and sugar are also made from crystals. Then there are the quartz crystals in your watch and the silicon in your computer.

GROW SOME CRYSTALS

1 Pour some hot tap water into a clean glass jar. Stir in one spoonful of potash of alum at a time.

2 Keep adding alum until no more will dissolve. You now have a *saturated solution*. Leave it for two days.

3 Drain the saturated solution through a strainer. Save the water for later and keep the crystals.

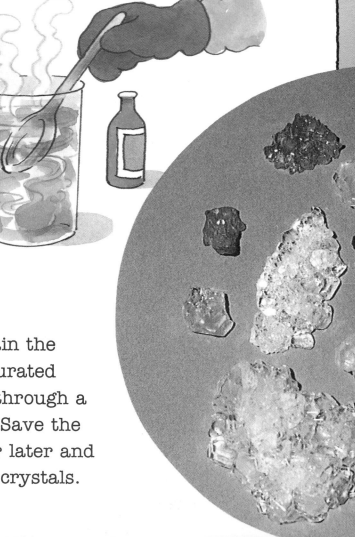

WHY IT WORKS

When the alum dissolved, the particles it was made up of spread out in the water. As the water evaporated, there was not enough water to dissolve the rest of the alum. The particles of alum were forced back together again to make crystals.

4 Look at the crystals with a magnifying glass. They are different sizes. Are they the same shape?

FURTHER IDEAS

Pour the spare saturated solution into a jar. Hang your crystals from a pencil and lower it into the jar. Watch it grow over a few days.

HANGING ROCKS

Rainwater can dissolve some types of solid rock. Sometimes the water drips into an underground cave, leaving a solid behind.
    Over time this solid slowly builds up to form columns, which hang down from the roof of the cave, called *stalactites*.

GROW A STALACTITE

1 Make a saturated solution with Epsom salts in a jar of hot water.

2 Fill two glasses with the saturated solution.

3 Attach paper clips to the ends of some wool. Hang the ends in the two glasses.

4 Place a saucer under the wool. Leave in a warm, safe place for the one week.

5 Watch as the stalactite grows down from the wool to the saucer, over a number of days.

WHY IT WORKS

The saturated solution soaks into the wool and spreads along its length. Some of it drips off the wool and onto the saucer. As it drips, the water evaporates, leaving behind a column of salts.

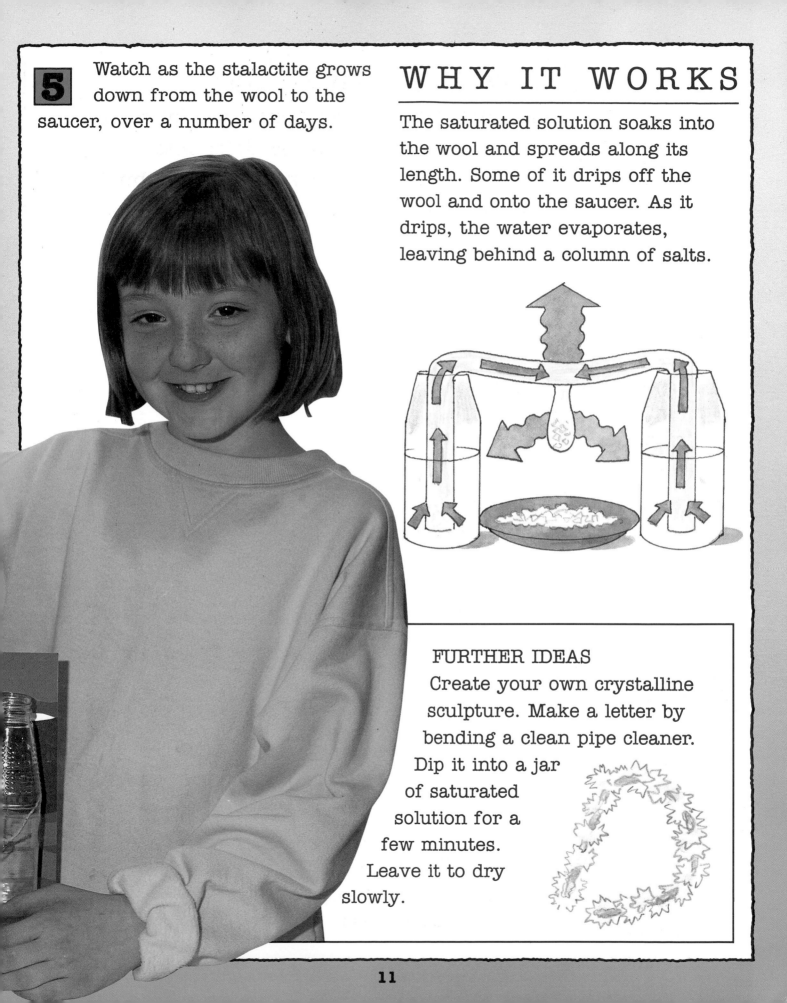

FURTHER IDEAS

Create your own crystalline sculpture. Make a letter by bending a clean pipe cleaner. Dip it into a jar of saturated solution for a few minutes. Leave it to dry slowly.

SHAPE AND STRENGTH

Everybody knows how easy it is to break an egg, because of its very thin shell. However, the egg can also be very strong. It must withstand the impact of falling to the ground when the egg is laid. The egg shape has been produced by nature to be both light and strong.

TEST THE STRENGTH OF AN EGG

1 Find a large tray. Stand up the egg at one side of the tray using clay to hold it in place.

2 At the other side of the tray place two piles of coins exactly the same height as the egg. The egg and two piles should make a triangle.

3 Wrap some books in plastic wrap for protection. Support one book on the coins and egg.

4 Add another book. Watch the egg carefully as you add each book. How many books can the egg help support before it breaks?

WHY IT WORKS

The shape of the egg makes it both hollow and light. It has an arch at each end, a good structure for supporting weight. The egg has a lot of strength lengthwise because the tall arches spread more weight. It is much easier to break when on its side because these arches are weaker.

FURTHER IDEAS
Repeat the test. This time compare the egg's strength to that of some paper shapes, such as a box and a cone.

HANGING AROUND

One of the most important properties of any material is its strength. A material that snaps under the slightest weight is not much use. Nature has made some of the strongest materials around. For example, the silken strands in a spider's web are stronger than steel of the same thickness.

FIND THE STRONGEST STRIP

1 Cut three strips of paper, tissue paper, and plastic from a plastic bag, making them the same length and width.

2 Using tape, fasten a wooden dowel to each end of the strips.

GET AN ADULT TO DO THIS FOR YOU

3 Ask an adult to cut two small holes on each side of the top of three paper cups, to make three baskets.

4 Attach a basket to one of the wooden dowels. Tie string around the other wooden dowel.

5 Hang each strip from a wall. Slowly add weights to the baskets until each strip breaks.

WHY IT WORKS

Plastic is the strongest because its particles are held together by very strong bonds. Paper is made from densely packed fibers that can be split apart quite easily. Tissue paper fibers are not as densely packed, making it the weakest of the three.

FURTHER IDEAS
Repeat the test with plastic strips of different widths. How does this affect the strength?

MAKING MATERIALS

The materials we find in nature are called *raw materials*. We use many of these and change them to make other products. Glass is made from sand, and paper from wood. We can usually improve a material by changing its properties.

MAKE A PAPIER-MÂCHÉ BOWL

1 Mix some flour and water in a large plastic bowl, keeping the mixture runny.

2 Tear up strips of newspaper, and soak them in the mixture.

3 Inflate a balloon. Starting near the balloon's middle, apply the soaked paper in layers.

4 To make the bowl's base, sit the balloon on a plastic lid. Cover the lid with more papier-mâché

5 Leave overnight, then remove the balloon. Paint the finished bowl for decoration. Varnish it for extra protection.

WHY IT WORKS

Paper is made up of thousands of tiny strands of wood fibers. The mixture of flour and water fills the gaps between these fibers. As the mixture dries it becomes hard and makes the paper strong and more rigid. It keeps its new shape until soaked again in water.

FURTHER IDEAS

You can use a real bowl as a mold. Cover the bowl with plastic wrap first to make the papier-mâché easy to remove.

FILLING SHAPES

Like papier-mâché, materials such as cement, plaster, and gypsum alter their form when mixed with water and allowed to dry. Unlike papier-mâché, these substances can be poured into molds and used to form shapes, from small statues to enormous buildings.

PLASTER OF PARIS

1 Lubricate the inside of a clean, rubber glove with a few drops of liquid soap.

2 Hang the glove upside down with a couple of clips to hold it open.

3 Use a wooden stick to mix some plaster of Paris with cold water in a glass jar. Mix thoroughly until creamy.

4 Pour the mixture into the glove. Make sure it is filled to the top.

5 Leave overnight to dry out. Gently peel off the glove from the plaster underneath. Be careful! The plaster is quite fragile.

6 Paint the plaster to brighten it up. Use your hand sculpture for holding jewelry.

WHY IT WORKS

Plaster of Paris is made by heating crushed gypsum. The water evaporates away leaving behind a dry powder. When you add water to this powder you cause a chemical reaction. The powder is changed back to gypsum, which will set hard when the water has evaporated.

FURTHER IDEAS
Hollow out the shape of a face in some clay. Pour plaster of Paris into the mold and leave it to dry overnight, making a plaster cast of the face.

ELASTIC MATERIALS

One of the reasons metals are so useful is because of their springiness, or *elasticity*. This means that as you pull the material out of shape it tries to return to that shape. Most things have some springiness, especially elastic bands, which are very strong. Glass is also strong, but instead of being elastic it is brittle and shatters.

MAKE A JACK-IN-THE-BOX

1 Ask an adult to coil a piece of stiff wire around a broom handle to make a spring.

2 Cut the neck from a plastic bottle. Attach the spring to the bottom with tape.

3 Ask an adult to secure a lid with paper fasteners.

GET AN ADULT TO DO THIS FOR YOU

4 Draw a "Jack" face on a Ping-Pong ball, push it into the box, and close the lid.

5 Open the box and see how far your "Jack" will fly!

WHY IT WORKS

Most materials can return to their original shape after being stretched. Metals are very good at this, especially when coiled into a spring. In a squashed spring each part of the metal pushes in order to return the spring to its original position. This force makes "Jack" jump out of the box.

FURTHER IDEAS
Cut out the outline of a frog twice, and stick them together. Attach a piece of elastic and hang it up, then pull and release it. Watch the frog bounce.

SHAPELESS PLASTICS

Some materials can be pulled into new shapes which they then keep. They do not return to their previous shape as an elastic material would. Such materials are called "plastic." For example, wet clay is plastic because you can mold it into any shape you want and it stays that way.

MAKE SOME PLASTIC MILK

1 Ask an adult to warm some milk in a pan.

2 When the milk starts to boil, slowly stir in a little vinegar.

GET AN ADULT TO HELP YOU WITH THESE

3 Keep stirring. Within seconds the mixture should become rubbery.

4 Let this rubbery mixture cool. Wash it under the cold water tap, and examine the "plastic."

WHY IT WORKS

Vinegar is a member of the chemical family called *acids*. When it is added to the warm milk, it sets up a chemical reaction which rearranges the particles in the milk. Instead of being "runny" and free to move, they clump together. It is this clump that becomes the lump of "plastic."

FURTHER IDEAS
Put a plastic container in a saucepan. Ask an adult to boil water. Pour the boiling water to cover the container, and watch it lose its shape.

FIBERS AND THREADS

Fibers are long, thin, flexible strands of material like threads. Each of your hairs is a fiber. Natural fibers also include animal fur, cotton, and wool. Fibers can be twisted together to make yarn, which can be woven in turn to make fabrics or cloth.

MAKE A LOOM

1 Cut an odd number of notches along the top and bottom of some cardboard.

GET AN ADULT TO DO THIS FOR YOU

2 Wind a piece of string around each pair of notches. Knot it together at the back of the loom.

3 Weave some thick wool across the loom, in and out of the string. To change color, tie another strip to the old one.

4 When you have filled the loom, tie off the last strip of fabric. Lift the weaving off the cardboard.

5 Push pieces of a dowel through the top and bottom warp threads. Hang it up as a decoration.

WHY IT WORKS

The strings going up and down are called the *warp threads*. The threads going across are called the *weft threads*. By weaving the threads together the finished fabric is strong. The closer the weave, the stronger the finished fabric.

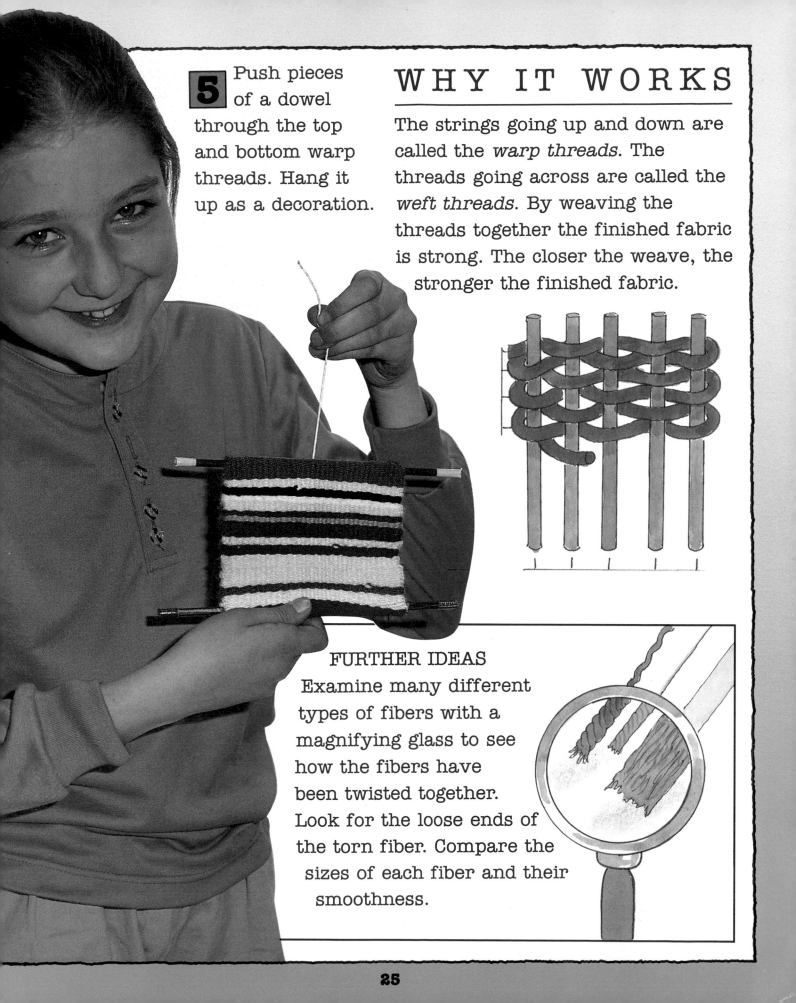

FURTHER IDEAS

Examine many different types of fibers with a magnifying glass to see how the fibers have been twisted together. Look for the loose ends of the torn fiber. Compare the sizes of each fiber and their smoothness.

FITTING IT TOGETHER

Some shapes fit neatly together to cover an area without overlapping or leaving spaces. This is called *tessellation*. Examples are the bricks in a wall and the squares on a chessboard. An example in nature is the honeycomb in a beehive, where hexagonal cells fit snugly together.

MAKE A TRIANGLE PUZZLE

1 On a large sheet of white cardboard, draw a triangle with sides 12 inches long.

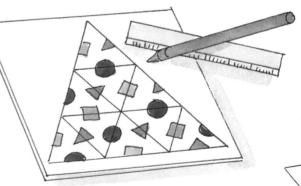

2 Divide the large triangle into nine smaller ones. Each side should be 4 inches long.

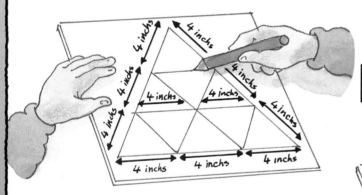

3 On each of the triangles draw a circle, a square, and a triangle as shown.

GET AN ADULT TO HELP YOU WITH THIS

4 Use sharp scissors to carefully cut out each of the nine small triangles.

WHY IT WORKS

A tessellated structure, like a beehive, must have no gaps or overlapping shapes. Only certain shapes, such as triangles and hexagons, will tessellate. To cover a surface with circles, which do not tessellate, you would have to overlap the shapes, or leave gaps.

5 Challenge a friend with your triangle puzzle. They should be able to match up the pattern to correctly put the big triangle back together again.

FURTHER IDEAS
A mosaic is like a tessellation, but the shapes that fit together are not the same. Cut out alot of small cardboard shapes. Glue them down to fit the outline of a drawing on cardboard. Make the gaps as small as possible.

BRIDGES

Since earliest times people have built bridges to cross rivers and other obstacles. The first bridges were probably tree trunks laid across a stream. Later, bridges were built from arches to carry heavier loads. Modern bridges use either steel girders or suspension cables, for support.

BUILD MODEL BRIDGES

1 Find six blocks of wood to make three bridges. Tape pencils to two of the corners on each block.

2 Ask an adult to cut some strips of thick cardboard the same width as the blocks.

GET AN ADULT TO HELP YOU WITH THIS

3 Place a strip of cardboard between two blocks to make a beam bridge. With the second, use an arch as a support.

4 On the third, tie string to the pencils, and tape the string to the strip to make a suspension bridge.

5 Draw a river on a sheet of cardboard. Place it under your bridges.

6 Place weights in the middle to test which bridge is the strongest.

WHY IT WORKS

The beam bridge is the weakest because the weight is not spread. The string in the suspension bridge takes some of the weight. The arch is strongest because the weight is spread out over its whole length.

FURTHER IDEAS
Try making a bridge frame out of plastic straws. Join the straws together by pushing the end of one into another.

FANTASTIC SHAPES FACTS

The longest stalactite in the world is 195 feet long and can be found in the Cueva de Nerja in Spain. The tallest stalagmite is only 105 feet high and is deep within the Krásnohorká Cave in Slovakia.

Diamonds are among the most valuable objects. The largest was discovered in South Africa in 1905. The Cullinan diamond, as it was called, was subsequently cut into 106 separate, polished stones.

The largest bird, the ostrich, lays the largest egg. Ostrich eggs are usually 8 inches long and can support a person weighing 280 pounds. In contrast, the egg of the hummingbird is 0.39 inches long and weighs under half a gram!

The longest cable suspension bridge can be found crossing the Humber estuary in England. It is 4,626 feet in length and its two towers stretch 533 feet above the water. It is so long that builders had to take into account the curvature of the Earth when the bridge was under construction.

Contrary to public opinion the Earth is not round. It is, in fact, shaped like a slightly squashed ball. The distance around the equator is just longer than the distance around the North and South Poles. The technical name for such a shape is an *oblate spheroid.*

Over millions of years, fish and other creatures that swim have developed a body shape which allows them to cut through the water with the minimum of effort. Their body shapes cut down drag, which would slow them down. Humans have learned from nature's design and have copied these streamlined shapes for boats and submarines.

Airplanes can fly because of the shape of their wings. They are made so that air flowing over the top of the wing travels faster than the air flowing below the wing. The result is that the wing and the plane are pushed upward into the air. The wings of birds, bats, and insects also use this principle to stay aloft.

GLOSSARY

Arch
A shape, roughly semicircular, that is capable of supporting a great deal of weight.

Brittle
When an object can be easily broken.

Crystal
A solid body in which the atoms are arranged in a rigid structure.

Elastic
An elastic object will recover its original shape after being molded.

Möbius strip
A surface that has only one side. It is made by joining the two ends of a strip that has been twisted around once.

Particle
A tiny piece of a substance.

Plastic
When a body can be shaped into a new form, it is said to be plastic. Its properties allow it to be molded and then retain its new shape.

Rigid
When an object is stiff and inflexible, it is said to be rigid. Its structure will not allow it to be bent or formed into any other shape.

Saturated
When a substance has been filled to its fullest possible extent.

Streamlined
The quality of a shape which allows it to travel through either air or water with minimum effort. It achieves this by not creating drag, which may slow a body down.

Structure
The arrangement of parts to form an entire object.

Tessellation
The ability of shapes to fit together neatly and cover an area without overlapping or leaving any spaces.

Weaving
To form a fabric by interlacing fibers. The weft threads are woven through the warp threads, to create the finished cloth.

INDEX

Acids 23
Alum 8, 9
Arch 13, 28, 29, 31

Balloon 17
Bridges 28-29, 30
Brittle 31

Coins 12, 13
Cotton 10
Crystals 8, 9, 10, 11,
   31

Diamonds 8

Earth 30
Eggs 5, 12, 13, 30
Elasticity 20, 21
Emeralds 8
Epsom salts 10, 11

Fabric 24, 25
Fibers 24, 25
Frog 21

Gemstones 8
Glass 16, 20
Gypsum 18, 19

Jack-in-the-box 20, 21

Milk 22, 23
Möbius strip 6, 7, 31
Mosaic 27

Paper 6, 7, 14, 16, 17, 21
Papier-mâché 16-17
Pencil 7, 28, 29
Plaster of Paris 18, 19
Plastic 14, 15, 22, 23, 31
Potash of alum 8, 9

Solution 8, 10, 11
Spring 5, 20, 21
Stalactites 10, 11, 30
Stalagmites 30
Straws 29
Streamlined 30, 31
Strength 12, 13, 14, 15, 28, 29

Tessellation 26, 27, 31
Threads 24, 25
Triangle puzzle 26, 27

Vinegar 22, 23

Warp 25, 31
Weaving 24, 25, 31
Weft 25, 31
Weight 28, 29
Wings 30